Published by: Jenoir Lynne'
Text copyright: The Beauty Institute

Printed in the United States of America. All rights reserved solely by the author. The author guarantees all contents are original. No parts of this book may be reproduced in any form without permission of the author.

No part of this publication may be reproached, stored in a retrieval system, or transmitted in any form or by any means, electronic, mechanical, photocopying, recording, or otherwise without the written permission of the author.

For information regarding permission, visit our website at www.entreprenewher.org or email us at info@entreprenewher.org

ISBN
979-8-9898177-3-3

Your new identity awaits...

Often times, as women, we tend to wrap our identity in the titles we've accumulated throughout life, the lies we were told about ourselves, and the trauma imprinted on us. While the roles we take on help to shape our existence, they are not our identity. The problem with these false identities is that if or when our positions and seasons shift or we no longer own these titles, we feel lost and unsure of who we are.

Our true identity lies in who God says we are. And, the beautiful thing about placing our identity in God is that He never leaves us, He never forsakes us, He never changes His mind about us. He is solid ground. Our identity is unwavering in Him.

Throughout this guide, you will discover Christ's true love for you and the identity He's given you through scripture.

Read your guide daily and say your affirmations to yourself in the mirror, out loud. Participate in the daily reflection writing prompt to further reinforce what you're learning.

And when you're done, re-read the scripture and affirmations as often as you need, to remind yourself of who you are. Make it a daily habit, share this book and what you're learning about identity with others.

Dismantling false identities

If anyone knows about the dangers of living life with a false identity, it's me.

I was born in Baltimore city to a single mother and a drug-addicted father. I knew who my father was but I didn't know him. He was never a consistent part of my life and very early on, I convinced myself that I didn't need him. In reality, this was a defense mechanism I used to mask the pain and void I felt from him not being there. I would often say, "I don't care" when he didn't show up to birthday parties and "my life is fine without him", with every award ceremony he missed.

This lie became even more ingrained in me when my mother got married and I now had a step dad. In my mind, he was going to replace my biological dad, the void would be filled, and life would be normal. But, even as amazing as my new dad was, the false identity I had taken on had already been rooted. This false identity of mine was, fatherless. The firm foundation, sense of security, and trust that I would be unconditionally loved and provided for was foreign to me. Even with a new father who displayed all of these things, I still yearned to get it from the man whom I inherited half my DNA from.

My fatherless identity showed up in everything I did. My friend-groups, the boyfriends I chose, the life paths I took. It bled into everything. I became a teen mom at 17 and when I was 23, I married my then boyfriend because I was pregnant with my second child and it seemed like the right thing to do. I stayed in that toxic marriage for 15 years. I had silently deemed myself unworthy of better.

The unhealthy rhythm in relation to a man felt normal to me because I operated from a fatherless identity. Until one day, God removed the scales from my eyes. Not that He had not revealed the toxicity of my marriage to me several times before, but this day it hit different. I sat in my garage, staring at a 15 year old journal entry that mirrored the exact state of my marriage at that current moment. The same core issues and emotional turmoil were still there. It hit me, almost like an out of body experience, "this is not going to change". All the hope I had in potential, the excuses of keeping the family together, the idea that things would get better with time; were all dismantled in that moment. I knew if I wanted to see change, I had to be the change and leave. That day I decided to end my 15 year marriage, for real this time.

Divorce is an unearthing experience. Everything you had clarity about regarding yourself and your future, now become the most unclear parts of your life. I found myself at rock bottom. I knew I had gotten myself into this. But I wanted to know how I got here so i'd never end up here, ever again. In a room, all by myself, I cried out "God, how did I get here?!" His response was unexpected and seemed unrelated, at first. He told me it was because of my daddy issues. And then He prompted me to write my biological father a letter. At this time, my father had already passed away due to health complications from addiction.

I'm thinking, "what does a letter to my dead father have to do with this, God?" But, I did it anyway. When I started the letter, I was angry and I aired my grievances to my father. But the more I wrote, the more God revealed to me that I was never fatherless at all and that He (God) was my father the entire time. I wept and felt a huge weight lift off of me. I released my fatherless identity and took on my rightful identity as daughter.

Not only was I daughter but a royal daughter, an heiress of the King of Kings. This identity had been there for me the whole time but, now I had taken ownership of it myself.

Your false identity may or may not be fatherless. Maybe it's "unworthy", "not enough", or "the outcast". Maybe it's something that stems from your child hood or rooted in trauma from a past relationship. Whatever it or they may be, it's time to dismantle the false identities. Knowing who you are and whose you are will determine how you show up in the world, the decisions you make, and the people you give access to you. Your identity influences everything you do. That's why it's so important to have our identity firmly rooted in Christ. Your God given identity will change your posture to upright and worthy. It gives you the necessary foundation of The Father. Because God is the one who created you and hand crafted your existence, only He can determine your true identity.

A note from the author

Dear Sister,

I wrote this guide with you in mind. The woman who's been searching for more, who senses there's purpose within her, yet sometimes wrestles with doubt, insecurity, or confusion about who she truly is. I was once that woman so I see you and I understand where you are.

Identify Her is more than a guide. It's a journey back to the heart of the One who created you.

Before the titles, the roles, and the expectations; you were known, seen, and called by name. God didn't just create you by chance. He designed you intentionally, wrapped you in purpose, and marked you with power.

As you journey through the pages over the next 30 days, my prayer is that you silence the lies you were told about yourself, release the weight of comparison, and embrace your true identity in Christ. It is time to rise as the woman God always intended you to be.

With love,
Jenoir Lynne'

First things first, let's write down all the false identities that come to mind.

Pray and ask God to reveal the root cause of your false identities and write down what He reveals to you.

Then we'll spend the next 30 days discovering your true identity in Him.

DAY 1

S M T W T F S

I AM

DATE: _____

Before I formed you in the womb I knew you,
and before you were born I consecrated you.

Jeremiah 1:5

How amazing is it to know that before you were even in your mother's womb, God knew you. He created you and deemed you sacred to Him. Thee Creator of all things, created YOU! He intricately designed you from your hair to your eyes to your toes and everything in between. He knew you before anyone else knew you. He knew your gifts, your temperament, your likes and dislikes. He still knows you now, even better than you know yourself.

Today's Affirmation
I am known by God. He knows every single part of me. I am special to Him.

How does it feel to know the depth of how much you are known by God? Write how you feel below:

DAY 2

S M T W T F S

I AM
chosen

DATE: _____

> The Lord your God has chosen you out of all the peoples on the face of the earth to be His people, His treasured possession.
>
> Deuteronomy 7: 6

God chose you long before the world began. Before He formed heaven and earth, He chose you. He hand-picked you to be His precious treasure and you belong to Him. Sometimes we seek to be chosen by people in the world but when God has already chosen you, no other validation can compare.

Today's Affirmation

I am God's treasured possession. I do not need to seek validation in other people or things. I am already chosen.

Knowing that you are already chosen by God and don't need to convince others to chose you, how will you show up differently in the world today?
How does being chosen by God make to feel?

I AM *loved*

DAY 3

S M T W T F S

DATE: _____

"The mountains may shake to pieces, and the hills may disappear. But I will never take my love away from you. My covenant that brings peace between us will never finish." That is what the Lord who is very kind to you says.

Isaiah 54:10

How wonderful it is to be loved by God. He shows His love for you daily. We can see His love in the smallest things throughout each day. His love is unwavering and promised to you, always.

Daily Affirmation

I am loved by the very creator of love. No one else could ever love me as much as God. His love is unconditional and never failing. I have an abundance of love in my life.

Think about a time when you felt most loved by God? Reflect on how His love is different than any other love on earth.

DAY 4
S M T W T F S

I AM

DATE: _____

"Because you are precious in my sight and honored, and I love you, I will give people in exchange for you and nations instead of your life."

Isaiah 43:4

God not only loves you but, He honors you. He admires the very work of His hands, which is you. He shows His honor for you daily in even the smallest ways, don't miss it.

Today's Affirmation

I am honored by the most high God. He has called me honorable, therefore, I am.

Reflection

Being honored by God means you are highly respected by Him. How will you show up today, knowing you're honored by God?

DAY 5

S M T W T F S

I AM

DATE: _____

You are altogether beautiful, my darling; there is no flaw in you.

Song of Songs 4:7

The beauty God created in you is not just your physical appearance. It's your heart, your mind, your being. He sees your beauty beyond what the world sees. In fact, He sees the most beautiful parts of you every day.

Daily Affirmation

I am beautiful inside and out. When people see me, they see the beauty of God.

Reflection

List all the wonderful & beautiful things about you:

_____
_____
_____
_____
_____
_____
_____
_____
_____
_____
_____
_____
_____
_____
_____
_____
_____
_____
_____
_____
_____

DAY 6

S M T W T F S

I AM

DATE: _____

I, only I, am He who wipes out your transgressions for My own sake, and I will not remember your sins.

Isaiah 43:25

How amazing is it that your sins have not only been forgiven, but also forgotten by The Father. Jesus died for our sins. He paid it all on the cross. Will you fully receive the gift of salvation and forgiveness?

Daily Affirmation

I am already forgiven by God and today, I choose to forgive myself too.

Reflection

Forgiveness is easy for God but it can sometimes be difficult for us. Think of the things you have not forgiven yourself for. Place your hand on your heart, close your eyes, breathe deeply, and say out loud (then write down) what you will forgive yourself for.

DAY 7

S M T W T F S

I AM
set apart

DATE: _____

Before I formed you in the womb I knew you,
before you were born I set you apart;

Jeremiah 1:5

God's plans for you have been intentional from the start.
He knew the unique design He had carved out for you.
He made you uniquely set apart for a divine purpose.

Daily Affirmation

I am unique and set apart. I embrace the way
God created me.

What if your "flaws" were created in you, on purpose? Well, guess what? They were. God makes no mistakes, even our flaws are by design. They serve a purpose in our lives. Reflect on reframing your flaws to see the benefit of them.

DAY 8

S M T W T F S

I AM
voice

DATE: _____ ♡

Now go, I will help you speak and teach you what to say.

Exodus 4:12

Even when you feel unqualified, God equips your voice. You *are* voice. You are the mouthpiece of heaven. The enemy attacks our voices at a young age in an attempt to delay and derail our purpose. But, God has designed you to use your voice to represent the kingdom. Adjust your crown, queen. Speak boldly.

Daily Affirmation

I am bold, I am fearless, I am voice.

Reflection

Where has your voice been silenced? What steps will you take now to reclaim your rightful voice?

I AM
an overcomer

DAY 9
S M T W T F S

DATE: _____

Who is (s)he who overcometh the world, but
(s)he that believeth that Jesus is the Son of God?

1 John 5:5

In life you face many battles, internally and externally. The good news is that the fight is fixed. God has already overcome the world and through your belief in Him, you have already overcome the world too. Rest assured that nothing takes your Father by surprise and He's already worked all things out in your favor.

Daily Affirmation

I am an overcomer. Everything I will ever face, has already been handled by God.

Reflection

Think about a challenge or circumstance that has brought on worry or anxiety? Now, think about how you will be victorious in the end. Write down, in faith, how God will give you the victory.

_____
_____
_____
_____
_____
_____
_____
_____
_____
_____
_____
_____
_____
_____
_____
_____
_____
_____
_____
_____

I AM
protected

DAY 10
S M T W T F S

DATE: _____

But the Lord is faithful, and He will strengthen you and protect you from the evil one.

2 Thessalonians 3:3

God is constantly protecting you, every single day. There are times where we witness His protection and see the danger He kept us from, right before our eyes. But, He's also protecting us beyond what we see. Sometimes that protection looks like delay or denial. We think we're missing out on something, but it's often a subtle way of God protecting his precious child.

Daily Affirmation

I am protected by my Father. He guides me each day. I am safe with Him.

Reflection

Write a "thank you" letter to God for the things you've seen Him protect you from. Give Him praise for the unseen things.

_____
_____
_____
_____
_____
_____
_____
_____
_____
_____
_____
_____
_____
_____
_____
_____
_____
_____
_____
_____
_____
_____

I AM
a masterpiece

DAY 11

S M T W T F S

DATE: _____ ♡

> For we are God's masterpiece. He has created us anew in Christ Jesus, so we can do the good things he planned for us long ago.
>
> Ephesians 2:10

You are a masterpiece, handcrafted by The Creator. Your intricate and well-thought-out design is specific to only you. God took His time to create you, place you, and order your footsteps. He takes pride in His creation. He takes pride in you.

Daily Affirmation

I am a divine masterpiece, created by The Master.

Think of your unique design. Reflect on how God uses the uniqueness of you to help others and advance the kingdom.

DAY 12

S M T W T F S

I AM

DATE: _____

See how much our Father loves us, for He calls us His children, and that is what we are!

1 John 3:1

Anytime we need a reminder of how our Father sees us as His daughters, we can look at a loving, healthy father-daughter relationship here on earth. This could be your personal relationship or one that you admire. Good fathers give limitlessly to their daughters; they spoil them and they are fulfilled in doing so. It's the same way with God. He is a perfect father. It gives Him great joy to be your father and spoil you too. He loves to care for, protect, and provide for you.

Daily Affirmation

There's nothing my Father won't do for me, according to His will. He loves me deeply. I am His daughter.

Think about a time when you felt the warm, fatherly love of God. Journal about it below:

DAY 13

S M T W T F S

I AM

kept

DATE: _____

Look at the birds. They don't plant or harvest or store food in barns, for your heavenly Father feeds them. Aren't you far more valuable to Him than they are?

Matthew 6:26

You are a kept woman in Christ. Scripture tells us that all of our needs will be met and we will lack nothing. Being kept by God means we don't have to hustle, grind, and out perform the next woman to achieve. Our heavenly Father freely gives to us. He aligns us and gives us favor to receive so that we can have rest and abide in Him, without toil.

Daily Affirmation

I am a kept woman in Christ. God is aligning me with resources and provision daily.

Reflection

Think about examples of how God has kept you recently. Reflect on how good He is and how grateful you are.

DAY 14

S M T W T F S

I AM

DATE: _____ ♡

And since we are His children, we are His heirs.

Romans 8:17 a

To be an heir means you have been granted the inheritance of God. Because you are His child and you have submitted yourself to Him, you get to reap the benefits of being part of the royal family. You will experience reward here on earth, but your greatest reward will be in heaven.

Daily Affirmation

I am royalty. I am an heiress of my heavenly Father.

Reflection

Now that you know you are an heir of God, how will you show up differently in your life? Ask yourself, "what would an heiress do?"

_____
_____
_____
_____
_____
_____
_____
_____
_____
_____
_____
_____
_____
_____
_____
_____
_____
_____
_____
_____
_____
_____

I AM
a new creature

DAY 15

S M T W T F S

DATE: _____

> Therefore if any (wo)man be in Christ, (s)he is a new creature: old things are passed away; behold, all things are become new.
>
> 2 Corinthians 5:17

Chances are that wherever you first encountered God, you're not still there. You've grown and you've been redeemed. Therefore, you have become a new woman in Christ. When we are navigating "the new", it's unfamiliar and we can feel like we don't even know ourselves anymore. But, God knows you well. He knows this new version of you and He has led you here. When you feel uncertain, ask Him who you are and He will reveal the mysteries of your new self, to you.

Daily Affirmation

I am new in Christ. My identity is rooted in Him. I am who He says I am.

Write down any questions you want to ask God about your new identity. Then take them to Him in prayer.

I AM
victorious

DAY 16

S M T W T F S

DATE: _____

For the Lord your God is the one who goes with you to fight for you against your enemies to give you victory.

Deuteronomy 20:4

You are victorious through faith. You are more than a conqueror, which means you can overcome any challenge, adversity, or temptation. Our victory is not based on our strength but on His grace and love for us. Not only does God fight for us, but He leads us to each triumph.

Daily Affirmation

I am victorious in everything I will face today.
Victory is my portion.

Write about a circumstance or situation where you are believing God will give you victory at the end of it. Write, in faith, how it will end victoriously.

DAY 17

S M T W T F S

I AM
a temple

DATE: _____ ♡

Do you not know that your bodies are temples of the Holy Spirit, who is in you, whom you have received from God? You are not your own.

1 Corinthians 6:19

Have you ever paused to meditate on the fact that your body is an actual temple. And not just any temple but a temple for God's Holy Spirit. Your body is sacred to God. That's why it's important for us to treat our bodies as temples by being mindful of what we eat, listen to, watch, how we speak, exercising for physical health, and keeping our bodies pure before Christ.

Daily Affirmation

My body is a temple. God trusts me to honor the temple He gave me and I will not let Him down.

Reflection

What will you do differently in your routine today now that you have taken on the identity of temple?

DAY 18

I AM
purposeful

S M T W T F S

DATE: _____

For we know that all things work together for
the good of those who love Him, who have
been called according to His purpose.

Romans 8:28

We all find ourselves questioning or searching for our
purpose at some point in life. When we are unclear on what
it is, all we have to do is pray and ask God to reveal it to us.
The beauty about being purposeful is that your purpose is
already on the inside of you. It's not something you have to
search for. Our purpose will always, in some way, serve
others and build the kingdom of God on earth.

Daily Affirmation

I am purposeful. God has given me a special
assignment in the earth that's just for me to fulfill.

What clues do you currently see in your life about your God-given purpose?

I AM

DAY 19
S M T W T F S

DATE: _____

As each has received a gift, use it to serve one another, as good stewards of God's varied grace.

1 Peter 4:10

God has given you unique gifts. Gifts are different from talent or skills that we learn to do. Our gifts are apparent very early in our lives and they come naturally. Each gift serves a purpose and they are necessary in the body of Christ. Remember, only you are able to do what you do, in the exact way you do it.

Daily Affirmation

I am gifted. My special gifts were given to me by God and I will use them in ways that honor Him.

What gifts were given to you by God? How can you steward them better to give them back to Him?

I AM
fearfully & wonderfully made

DAY 20
S M T W T F S

DATE: _____ ♡

I praise you because I am fearfully and wonderfully made;
your works are wonderful,
I know that full well.

Psalm 139:14

Your life was created through a reverent and holy process. You are the result of an intentional act of God. Nothing about you is random. He created you, just the way He wanted you to be- meaningfully.

Daily Affirmation

I am fearfully and wonderfully made by God; thee creator of heaven and the universe. He took His time making me.

What are your favorite parts of yourself that God designed?

_____
_____
_____
_____
_____
_____
_____
_____
_____
_____
_____
_____
_____
_____
_____
_____
_____
_____
_____
_____
_____
_____
_____

DAY 21

S M T W T F S

I AM
appointed

DATE: _____

From one man He made all the nations, that they should inhabit the whole earth; and He marked out their appointed times in history and the boundaries of their lands.

Acts 17:26

The era in which you were born is no accident. Neither is the country and city you were born in. God orchestrated the large and small details of your creation and location, because you fulfill a need in the earth. Never forget that.

Daily Affirmation

I am appointed for this time and this place.
Thank you God for assigning me exactly where
i'm needed.

Reflection

Make a list of the proof you've seen of why God appointed you for the times and places in your life.

_____
_____
_____
_____
_____
_____
_____
_____
_____
_____
_____
_____
_____
_____
_____
_____
_____
_____
_____
_____
_____
_____
_____

DAY 22

S M T W T F S

I AM
an intentional creation

DATE: _____

For you formed my inward parts; you knitted me together in my mother's womb.

Psalm 139:13

Even if your birth was not the intention of your parents, you were always God's plan. Before anyone ever knew you existed, God knew. And, He rejoiced. No matter what you or anyone else may think, you are not a mistake. Your birth was not coincidental, nor was it the sole doing of your parents. God intentionally created you.

Daily Affirmation

I am an intentional creation of God. I belong. I was created with purpose.

Reflection

What lies have you believed about your coming into the world? Pray and ask the Holy Spirit to help you identify each lie. Then write down the truth to replace the lies.

DAY 23

S M T W T F S

I AM
redeemed

DATE: _____ ♡

In Him we have redemption through His blood, the forgiveness of sins, in accordance with the riches of God's grace.

Ephesians 1:7

You have received the most beautiful gift of redemption. You have been saved from your sin and the full penalty of it. Jesus paid for our sins and cleared our debt. Redemption is yours.

Daily Affirmation

I am redeemed. Jesus paid it all on the cross for me.

Reflection

Think about how gracious God has been to give you the gift of redemption. What areas in life has God redeemed you?

DAY 24

I AM
rich

S M T W T F S

DATE: _____

The blessing of the Lord makes a person rich, and He adds no sorrow with it.

Proverbs 10:22

No matter what those credit card balances and bills say, you are rich. To be rich in the Lord means to be blessed. You are rich because of God's provision and mercy, He has freely given you.

Daily Affirmation

I am rich. Provision and blessings chase after me daily.

Make a list of the riches God has given you. Remember not to
only list worldly possessions, but the intangible ones too
(health, favor, peace, etc)

DAY 25

S M T W T F S

I AM

DATE: _____

I will restore you to health and heal your wounds.

Jeremiah 30:17

Even when we are at our lowest, God can still heal and restore us. And, He always knows the perfect way to go about it. Sometimes we experience immediate healing and other times He takes us through a journey of healing. The first step is asking the Father to heal you. He will.

Daily Affirmation

I am healed in Christ. I am restored.

Reflection

Write God a letter or prayer asking Him for the healing you need. He's waiting for the invitation..

DAY 26

S M T W T F S

DATE: _____

It is the Lord who goes before you. He will be with you; He will not leave you or forsake you. Do not fear or be dismayed.

Deuteronomy 31:8

You are not alone. It may feel like it at times but your heavenly Father is always walking with you. Through every season, every day, every moment. He promised to always be with you and He is a man who can not lie.

Daily Affirmation

I am not alone. God is always with me. I have priority access to His presence.

Pray and ask God to allow you to tangibly feel His presence today. Take note of what He shows you. And remember to not limit God, His presence is everywhere.

DAY 27

S M T W T F S

I AM
rooted

DATE: _____

Then Christ will make His home in your hearts as you trust in Him. Your roots will grow down into God's love and keep you strong.

Ephesians 3:17

In life, we can sometimes find ourselves rooted in things of the world. Like, our self image, our financial status, or the labels others placed on us before we knew who we were. The good news is that God gives us an open invitation to be rooted in Him. All we have to do is trust Him.

Daily Affirmation

I am rooted in Christ. I trust You, Lord. I am who You say I am.

In what areas have you found yourself rooted in things of the world? What steps will you take to become more rooted in Christ?

I AM
a conqueror

DAY 28

S M T W T F S

DATE: _____

No, in all these things we are more than conquerors through Him who loved us.

Romans 8:37

Being a conqueror means you will overcome your adversary, the enemy. Those whispers of false identity are defeated. God has given you power to trample them under your feet.

Daily Affirmation

I am a conqueror. I have the power to overcome my adversaries.

Reflection

Think about the things you've conquered by God's grace. Write a list below to remind yourself that you are a conqueror.

DAY 29

S M T W T F S

I AM

DATE: _____ ♡

You are the light of the world. A city set on a hill cannot be hidden. Nor do people light a lamp and put it under a basket, but on a stand, and it gives light to all in the house. In the same way, let your light shine before others, so that they may see your good works and give glory to your Father who is in heaven.

Matthew 5:14-16

There is light inside of you. In fact, you are light. God's Holy Spirit shines through you. So, don't you dare shrink yourself to fit into dark spaces. You illuminate the darkness of this world, so that people can see God's love and light through you.

Daily Affirmation

I am the light of the world. I will let my light shine unapologetically.

Reflection

Write about the places God has called or may be calling you to bring light in your sphere of influence?

DAY 30

S M T W T F S

I AM
the salt of the earth

DATE: _____

You are the salt of the earth, but if salt has lost its taste, how shall its saltiness be restored? It is no longer good for anything except to be thrown out and trampled under people's feet.

Matthew 5:13

You are called by God to impact others on earth. Being the salt of the earth means you are the living example of God's word being lived out loud. Studying God's word, seeking Him in all things, and praying for yourself and others, are ways you can be the salt He's declared you to be.

Daily Affirmation

I am the salt of the earth. I am an example of God's word, personified.

Reflection

What ways do you already see yourself acting as the salt of the earth? In what areas can you improve?

YOU *did it!*

You devoted yourself to spending 30 days discovering your true identity in Christ and you did it! I am proud of you! My prayer is that you've not only gained insight, but that you've encountered the unwavering love of Christ in a deeply personal way. You were never meant to live confined by the expectations of the world or defined by your past. Your true identity is found in the One who created you — fearfully, wonderfully, and intentionally.

Remember, your worth is not measured by titles, accomplishments, or approval from others, but by the unchanging truth that you are a daughter of the King. You are seen, known, and loved beyond measure.

This is not the end — it's a beginning. A beginning of living from a place of wholeness, of walking boldly in your God-given identity, and of becoming the woman He designed you to be.

Stay rooted in His Word. Stay connected to His heart. And never forget: You are chosen. You are called. You are enough — because He is enough in you.

Now, go and live it.

Xo, Jenoir Lynne ♡

New identity

Write a letter to yourself about your newfound identity.

Those who receive Jesus and believe in His name are given the right to become children of God, and this *new birth* is not of blood, flesh, or human will, but of God.

John 1:12-13

Revelations on this journey...

Journal

www.ingramcontent.com/pod-product-compliance
Lightning Source LLC
Chambersburg PA
CBHW060420050426
42449CB00009B/2055